Donata Montanari

Children
Around the World

Kids Can Press

A World Full of Children

The world is very big.
It is filled with children.

There are children with black hair,
blond hair, red hair and brown hair.

There are children with dark skin,
light skin and colors in between.

Children wear clothes of many colors —
green overalls, yellow dresses, purple running shoes
and blue sweaters with stars.

In Tibet, young Buddhist
monks wear red robes.

In Mongolia, children tie yellow
sashes around their waists.

Masai girls of Africa have
necklaces made of tiny colored beads.

Children everywhere have
families and friends.
They like to play
and go to school,
just like you.

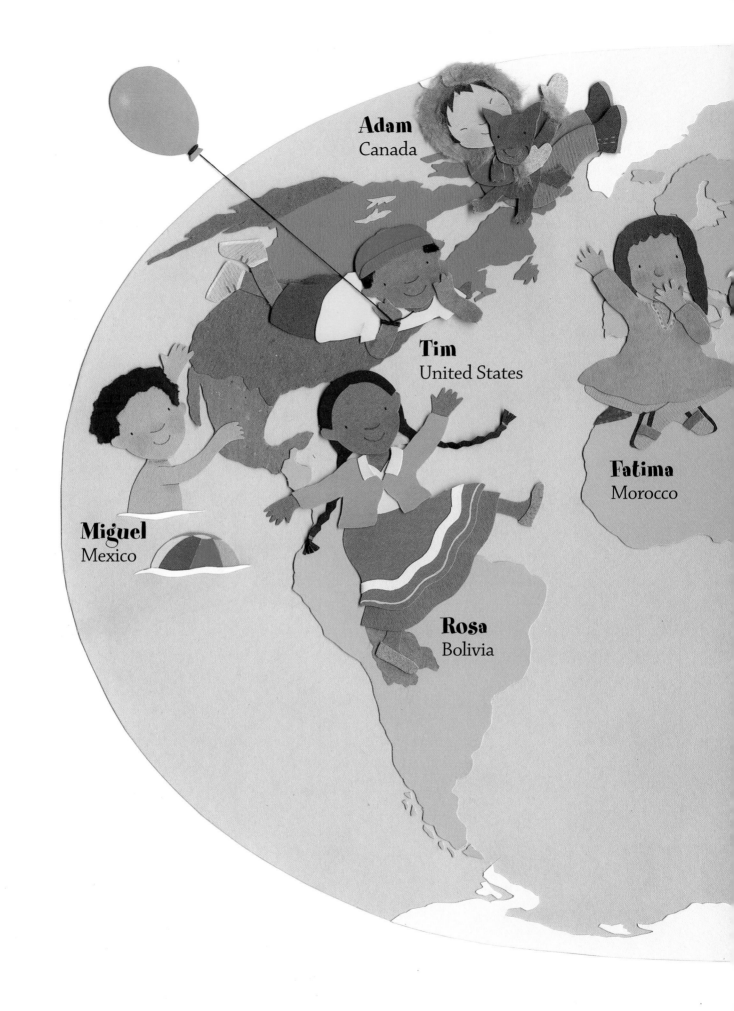

Adam
Canada

Tim
United States

Miguel
Mexico

Rosa
Bolivia

Fatima
Morocco

Ming Chan
China

Deepa
India

Stavros
Greece

Sadako
Japan

Malaika
Tanzania

Emilio
Philippines

Cathy
Australia

Come and meet these children from around the world.

Hi! I'm Emilio from the Philippines.

My country is made up of islands — 7000 of them.
My island is the most beautiful of all.
It is never cold here.
But summer is a rainy season.
It rains for three months!

My mother and father have a rice farm.
Growing rice is a lot of work.
We eat rice every day.

My father catches fish in the ocean.
Sometimes, I help him fish,
but during the week I go to school.

I have a little pet chicken.
His name is Pépé.
I hope he won't end up in the
cooking pot like the other chickens!

Hi! I'm Malaika from Tanzania.

I live in Tanzania, in East Africa.
It is always hot here in my village.
I speak Swahili at home.
I like to wear colorful clothes.
I wear my best clothes on Sundays
when I go to church.

My father works in the big city.
When he is away, he sends us letters.
I read them with my mother and my sister.
It feels as if he is here with us.

In our school, big children and
little children all learn together.
We are studying English.
I know my ABCs already!

Sometimes, my older sister does my hair
in tiny braids with beads on the ends.

Hello! I'm Ming Chan from China.

I live in Beijing.
It is a very big city.
Once, I went to see the Great Wall!
I speak Mandarin Chinese.
At school, I am learning to write.

We write with characters.
They are a little bit like pictures.
By the time I am big,
I need to know thousands of characters.

My mother and father
ride bicycles to work.
I have a bike, too.
I like to race with my friend.

My favorite lunch is shrimp and
steamed dumplings with rice.
I use chopsticks to eat.

My mother was born under the sign of the Dragon.
I was born under the sign of the Tiger.
That means I am very brave!

Hi! I'm Cathy from Australia.

I live on a farm in New South Wales.
I learned to ride a horse when I was very small.
My horse's name is Dave.
He is gentle and he loves carrots.

My parents raise sheep.
There are sheep everywhere!

In Australia, we have animals you cannot find
anywhere else in the world —
the kangaroo, the wombat, the koala bear.

Sometimes, I go to town with my parents.
I really like the lights and the shops.
But all that noise gives me a headache.
At the farm, it is always quiet.
I like it here best.

Hi! I'm Adam from Canada.

I live way up north, in Nunavut.
Nunavut is a territory of Canada.
The North Pole is in Nunavut!
I am Inuit.
Inuit means "the people."

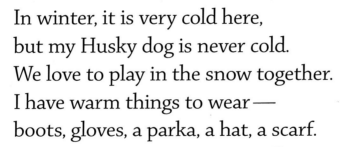

In winter, it is very cold here,
but my Husky dog is never cold.
We love to play in the snow together.
I have warm things to wear —
boots, gloves, a parka, a hat, a scarf.

My mother buys food at the grocery store.
My father likes to hunt for seals.
When he is far from home,
he builds an igloo to keep warm.
When I am bigger, he will teach me how!

I live in a house made of wood.
At home, we speak Inuktitut.
At school, my class is making a Web site.

Hello! I'm Fatima from Morocco.

Morocco is in northern Africa.
I live in Casablanca.
If you fly over my city,
the houses look like little white cubes.

In the summer,
my sisters and I sleep on the terrace.
It is lovely.
We can see the stars!

My family is Muslim.
We say prayers at home
and at the mosque.
When my mother goes out,
she covers her face with a veil.

For refreshment, we drink mint tea.
My mother bakes really good cookies.
She makes them with hazelnuts, walnuts and pistachios.

Hi! I'm Tim from the United States.

I live in New York City.
It is full of skyscrapers.
People call it "The Big Apple."
I like to go to the park with my friends.
We play basketball and go in-line skating.

My parents both work in offices.
They come home at six o'clock at night.
When they are not here, Mandy stays with me.
She is my babysitter.

Mom and Dad do not want me to watch
too much television,
but I can play computer games.
Mandy fixes my snack —
a peanut butter sandwich.

I live on the thirty-first floor of my building.
It feels like the top of the world!
I can see the whole city from the window.

Hello! I'm Deepa from India.

My city is called Varanasi.
The Ganges River runs through it.
My family is Hindu.
To us, the Ganges River is sacred.
Many, many people come to visit Varanasi.
They bathe in the river
and visit the temples.

I live in a brick house by the river.
My mother makes delicious meals
for me and my little brother.
My favorite is curried vegetables
and a flat bread called chapati.

My mother is a weaver.
When I am not at school,
I help sell her fabrics at the market.
Women buy them to make dresses called saris.
When I am big, I want to be a weaver, too!

Hi! I'm Miguel from Mexico.

I live in Mexico City,
and I speak Spanish.
It is mostly sunny and warm here.
I like to visit the market on Saturdays.
They sell ponchos and
lots of hot chilis.

When I come home from school,
I eat my lunch.
My mother makes tortillas with cheese,
beans and a spicy sauce called salsa.
My father is a dentist.
He eats with us, too.
After lunch, he takes a siesta.

Last summer, we went to the ocean.
We saw tourists from all over the world.
I loved swimming with the fish!

Hi! I'm Sadako from Japan.

Japan is a country made up of islands.
I live in the city of Osaka.
It is on the big island in the middle.

I eat with chopsticks.
My favorite food is raw fish.
It is called sushi when it is rolled with rice
and sashimi when it is only fish.
Yummy!

I sleep on a mattress called a futon.
At night, I unroll it on the floor.
In the morning, I roll it up and put it away.

My mother wears pants and sweaters,
but my grandmother wears kimonos.
She gave me one for my birthday!

I like video games and comic books.
In Japanese, comic books are called manga.

Hello! I'm Stavros from Greece.

I live near a village in the mountains.
We keep goats on our farm.
My father makes goat cheese called feta.
It is delicious.

Every morning, I go to school.
The teacher reads us stories about ancient heroes.
My favorite hero is Hercules.

I have one brother and two sisters.
We like to watch television.
We cheer for our favorite team!

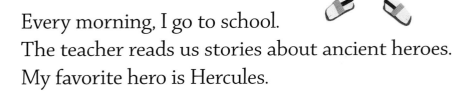

For a holiday, we go to the beach.
My grandparents always come along.
My mother packs a picnic
with tomato salad and feta cheese.
We play in the sand
and watch the boats sail by.

Hello! I'm Rosa from Bolivia.

My country is in South America.
I am an Aymara Indian.
I live in a village in the mountains
beside Lake Titicaca.

My father makes boats out of reeds.
Grandfather taught him how.
I want to learn, too.

My mother looks after our sheep and our llama.
Every day, she takes them up the hill to graze.

With my brother, I speak Aymara.
In school, we are learning Spanish.

My aunt lives in the big city, La Paz.
When she visits, we have a party.
We play music and dance.

More and More Children

Meet Ahmed, who lives in Egypt,
near the pyramids,
and Chinda from Thailand,
who loves to dance.

Here is Kiri,
who lives in New Zealand.
From her front porch,
she watches the dolphins in the sea.

This is Helena, who lives in Poland
and plays the violin.

The world is very big.
It is filled with children.

Many children in many places —
many things to do, many things to learn.

If you want to meet more children,
hop on the rainbow
and fly around the world!

Text © 1998 R.C.S. Libri S.p.A, Milan Italy
Illustrations © 1998 R.C.S. Libri S.p.A, Milan Italy
English text © 2001 Kids Can Press Ltd.
English translation by Yvette Ghione

Kids Can Press acknowledges the financial support of the Government of
Ontario, through the Ontario Media Development Corporation's Ontario
Book Initiative; the Ontario Arts Council; the Canada Council for the Arts;
and the Government of Canada, through the BPIDP, for our
publishing activity.

Published in Canada by
Kids Can Press Ltd.
25 Dockside Drive
Toronto, ON M5A 0B5

Published in the U.S. by
Kids Can Press Ltd.
2250 Military Road
Tonawanda, NY 14150

www.kidscanpress.com

The artwork in this book was rendered in paper collage.
The text is set in Chaparral.

Edited by Christine McClymont
Designed by Marie Bartholomew

The hardcover edition of this book is smyth sewn casebound.
The paperback edition of this book is limp sewn with a drawn-on cover.
Manufactured in Tseung Kwan O, NT Hong Kong, China, in 1/2012 by Paramount Printing Co. Ltd.

CM 01 0 9 8 7 6 5 4 3
CM PA 04 20 19 18 17 16 15 14 13 12 11

National Library of Canada Cataloguing in Publication Data

Montanari, Donata
        Children around the world / Donata Montanari.

Translated from Italian.
ISBN 978-1-55337-064-2 (bound)
ISBN 978-1-55337-684-2 (pbk.)

1. Children — Social life and customs — Juvenile literature.
2. Manners and customs — Juvenile literature. I. Title.

GT85.M6613 2001   j390'.083   C2001-930490-0